BYGONE

WHITEHAVEN

Volume Two

*A photographic look at life in Whitehaven and Cleator Moor
over the last one hundred years*

by

MICHAEL AND SYLVIA MOON

Published by
MICHAEL MOON
at
The Beckermet Bookshop
Beckermet
Cumbria

For Louisa Anne

I.S.B.N. 0904131-08-4

Design concept – Michael Moon

Design development and supervision – Keith Galliford

Printed in Great Britain by
The Scolar Press Limited, Ilkley, Yorkshire.

INTRODUCTION

When we compiled and published our first selection of local photographs we did not anticipate the worldwide response to our efforts which the book received. It has sold consistently all over the world since 1973. We hope that this second volume will give the reader as much pleasure as it has given us to compile it. We feel that Whitehaven has had an historically fascinating, though sometimes ignominious, past and we are looking forward to seeing the town rise again like a phoenix from amidst the demolished and ruined scars left over from the last century. These photographs are, again, our own selection, in which we are trying to portray a balanced view of what life was really like in the town when our grandparents were young. More material turns up periodically and we may, if demand warrants it, produce a third volume in the future. This depends largely on you, the reader, who may have, in your cupboard, attic or chest of drawers, old photographs and post-cards which are small, but important parts of this historical jigsaw puzzle which is Whitehaven's past.

Michael and Sylvia Moon,
March 1976.

ACKNOWLEDGMENTS

We wish to acknowledge with gratitude gifts of encouragement, advice and photographs from Daniel Hay, formerly Whitehaven Librarian; Harry Fancy and his staff at the Museum; David Andrews and his staff at Whitehaven Library; John Canavan; Bob Matthews; W. O'Pray; Mrs. M. Rooney; the Dyson family; Bob McLaughlin; G.A. Staples; Mr. Roan; Mr. R. Gill; Mr. A. Hailey, and Mr. and Mrs. E. Jordan.

Our very special thanks go to four people whose profound local know-ledge and good memories have helped to fill the many gaps in our researches — Mrs. Ida Parish, Bill Skelly, 'Spike' McLaughlin and Richard Bewsher.

To Ian Kyle we offer our thanks for some speedy and efficient photo-copying, and to David Swift, for his work on the Watson Collection for the library.

Finally, to Leonard Russell and John Hadfield, editors of the *Saturday Book,* who sowed the seeds of photographic nostalgia in us many years ago, when we borrowed their books from the library.

FOREWORD

by
Harry Fancy, Curator, Whitehaven Museum

The pen may be mightier than the sword, but the camera is faster than the pen! A single photograph can depict a place or an event more accurately and more directly than pages of written description, but pictures do have their limitations. From an historical point of view, they are of little value unless accompanied by certain basic facts — place, date, occasion etc., and the captions provided in this collection are a tribute to the authors' tenacity in seeking information even from the most unlikely places; certainly they are all that could be desired by the general reader.

Like its predecessor, this second book of photographs of Whitehaven sheds an invaluable sidelight on people and their varied ways of life in this facinating Cumbrian town. Many of the illustrations were selected from the Museum's growing collection of Copeland photographs, and we were delighted to have been able to provide some of the information for certain of the captions. Publications of this kind illustrate the importance of preserving photographs in a public Museum: all too often do we hear of irreplaceable photographs, negatives, magic lantern slides and postcards having been discarded by the relatives of people who may have cherished them for decades. Should you wish to donate or loan pictures of local interest for copying purposes, or if you know of the existence of such pictures, please contact

The Curator,
Whitehaven Museum,
The Market Hall,
Whitehaven,
Cumbria.
Telephone Whitehaven 5679.

1

1 Lowther Street, Winter 1895. As pretty as a scene on a Christmas Card! This is a view of Lowther Street, the town's main artery for nearly 300 years, from the Castle. Notice the high walls, iron gates and gatekeeper's lodge. When this picture was taken, the grounds were still part of a private house, lived in only occasionally by the Lowther family. The gates and lodge are down now and the walls have been substantially lowered to give access to the spacious and well laid out parklands. The Corporation bought the Castle in 1925, and after some structural alterations it became the town's hospital, replacing the old Infirmary in Howgill Street. It was opened by Princess Mary, Viscountess Lascelles, in January 1926.

2

2   Upper King Street, 1904.   At the turn of the century, photographers were not common, and many of the people have stopped to watch this one at work with his tripod, camera and black cloth cover. In those days, when buses and cars were rare, it was quite safe for the crowd to stand at what is now a busy road junction. Thankfully, King Street is now being made a pedestrian precinct so it will be safe once more.

The shop on the corner left, No. 64 King Street, is George Cowin's shop (formerly Holloway's, founded in 1853) with its fine display of brush heads round the door and with china figures and sets of milk jugs in the window. Francis Holloway was originally a brush maker, and toys later became an additional part of his business, the part for which he is best remembered. The building was taken down in the late 1930's and, in 1938, Burton's Tailors rebuilt on the site. The building beyond, on the same side, with its carved lion high up on the wall, is the Black Lion, an old established family and commercial hotel, which advertised in 1891 that "Bus and porter meet all trains", and that it had a "good Billiard room" — the equivalent amenity to a colour TV today. Note the Victorian folding pram on the extreme right of the picture.

3

3   Lower King Street.   Lower King Street, taken at the same time as the previous photograph and still causing the populace to lean on the stobs to watch the photographer with a critical eye. It must have been a summer's day — the little girls are wearing their big straw hats and some of the men are sporting their straw boaters. (In 1847, Whitehaven could support twelve straw hat makers). The four shops on the right were only pulled down about 7 years ago providing the town with one of its ugliest eyesores — a weed overgrown space and a fence which recent gales blew down.

W. B. Dalzell, the butcher at No. 41, toured the surrounding district with a cart twice weekly. "A postcard will bring us to your door" was one of their slogans. The shop window is of the sash type which could be raised to show off the wares, and the iron bars above would accommodate game birds and fowl, especially at Christmas. Further up the street, on the same side, were Dalzell's Tobacconists, the Billiard Hall, Borrowdale's Outfitters and Piper's Penny Bazaar with its open roller front and raised sloping counters on three sides.

4   Duke Street, 1939.   This view of houses and shops situated opposite the Dolphin will come as a surprise to many younger readers. This block was demolished in 1939 to widen Duke Street and to give access to the top of St. Nicholas' Graveyard which was later re-arranged into an ornamental garden. The headstones were laid flat and the railings seen on the left were removed, probably during the war.

The close proximity of these Georgian houses to the graveyard must have presented a health hazard in Victorian times, especially as it was vastly overcrowded due to gross over use before the new Town Cemetery was opened in 1855. The St. Nicholas' Graveyard had been in constant use since 1696 and there was great difficulty in finding a place in which to put another coffin. The number of funerals in the years 1841 — 48 was 1214, far in excess of the normal death rate, due mainly to typhus fever, caused by bad housing, gross overcrowding, lack of sewers and contaminated water supplies. We have a lot to be thankful for nowadays.

6

6　Whitehaven Market Place 1904.　The traditional meeting place and centre of business activity in the town was, and still is, the Market Place. In the immediate foreground is the Green Market with its iron stobs. The cast iron lamp post, a familiar landmark, has gone, but the stobs remain. In the past, the shops stayed open much later at night than nowadays, and 'Spike' McLaughlin tells us that 70 years ago his mother would send him, at 11.30 on Saturday night, with a pillow-case to old Charlie Greaves for 2 penn'orth of pot herbs. She would put it in a gypsy pan and make broth to feed her 10 children. The soup would last for a few days and the neighbours usually got a taste too.

The Cocoa Rooms, or the Coffee Shop as it was more usually known, where Walter Willson's supermarket is now, was the 'Wimpy Bar' of its day – a place where you could buy Pork Pies for 2d and 3d and a cheap hot drink. A firm local favourite, Bill Skelly tells us, was Nelson Cake, a sort of fruit madeira. A big lump cost ½d and a very big piece was 1d. It was very filling!

The Market Hall used to show Edisonia Films upstairs. Access was by a door and stone steps at the right hand side of the building – the steps up to the new Museum. The hoardings can be seen on the front of the building.

5　Sir James Lowther's Tomb.　This photograph was taken in Holy Trinity Church, Scotch Street, before its demolition in 1949. Sir James Lowther contributed £100 to the building of the church which cost £2,075. Sir James died, a bachelor, at his London home on 6th January 1755, at the age of 81. Although nicknamed 'Farthing Jemmy' due to his enterprise and frugality, he left a fortune of £600,000, a sum equal to several million pounds today, thus making him one of the richest commoners in England.

7

7   Market Place 1906.   This is another view of the Market Place on a quieter day in 1906. Notice Walker's milk float in the foreground and the little wooden cubicles in between the buttresses of the Market Hall which were shops. The end one on the right sold meat and was run by a man who worked for Billy Wilson, and Mrs. Preston kept the middle one. The marks where the roofs were fixed into the buttresses can still be seen by the observant passer-by. The shop on the left, No. 51, was Bewick's second hand book shop and barbers — an unusual combination of trades. J. Ramsay ran a grocers shop next door and the Pineapple's Off-Licence was beyond.

8

8   The Pow Beck Culvert under repair, 1927. The Pow Beck runs underground through the Market Place. Until 1764 it was an open stream crossed by three bridges, one opposite Dixon's Fish Shop, another by the Golden Lion and a third in front of the Y.M.C.A. in Irish Street. It would be used for dumping rubbish and made the arrangements of market stalls a little different from nowadays.

   This picture was taken in front of T. Watson's Joiners Shop in Strand Street, where the Electric Board building is now. At this point the stream descends by 10 steps, each 8" deep, covered by a 9 ft. wide archway. Another covered culvert runs under Duke Street, though it is of a different shape, being much wider and very shallow.

9 Scotch Street, 1858, taken from a Stereoscopic Slide. The basic street shape has not altered at all. The building on the left, now a solicitor's office, was once the home of Isaac Littledale, an unsuccessful contestant in the reform election of 1832. It was built before 1790. The buildings on the right were probably parts of a mansion house built about 1716 by a prominent local merchant named Walker Lutwidge, and were demolished to make way for two churches. Compare the difference with the next picture.

9

10

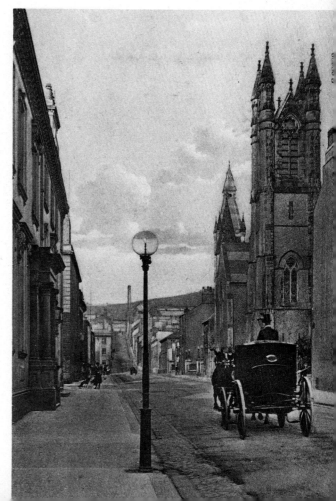

10 Here we can see, in this 1909 postcard, the two churches which were erected within a few years of each other, each trying to sport a higher tower. The church in the distance, the Congregational Church, was built in 1875 at a cost of £10,800 to seat 850 persons. It ceased being used as a church in the late 1960's, and has been used as a paint supermarket since, though now it looks as though it will be demolished. It had a fine granite marble columned porch which was removed, the pillars now forming part of a patio at the old Tower Brewery building on Inkermann Terrace.

The church on the corner, the Wesleyan Methodist, was built in 1879 at a cost of £11,000. A Gothic Style Church, built of granite with freestone facings, it affords 900 sittings. In the foreground of the picture is a funeral coach. Spikes were fixed on the back of some coaches to stop small boys climbing on for free rides which occasionally proved fatal when they fell off.

11 Lord Sangar's Circus used to pay regular visits to the town before the first world war and always caused a stir by parading with the menagerie through the town, up Tangier Street, through Branty Arch, turning round in front of the Grand Hotel, back across the town and through the Ginns to the Pottery Field where the Big Top was erected. Here we can see the elephants going up and the caged lions coming down.

11

12

12 Grand Hotel Passenger Footbridge, 1925. This picture is taken through the Bransty Archway, Tangier Street, looking towards the railway station. Beyond Mr. Meageen's 'bus, with its solid top and glass windows, can be seen the railway footbridge which allowed the speedy transfer of passengers and luggage from incoming trains to the Grand Hotel without having to worry about the weather.

12

13 & 14   Bransty Arch, Tangier Street, 1927.   This ancient structure, known as Bransty Arch, was built about 1800 to facilitate the removal of coal on a wooden railway laid from James Pit, over Tangier Street, and into a large staith on the dockside. Its threatened removal became an election issue in 1927, when Mr. W. Walker unsuccessfully petitioned for it to stay. The stone bridge was supposedly hindering traffic flow and was thought unsafe. It was taken down by erecting a wooden 'centre' which kept the roadway clear as work progressed. The cement holding the ashlar stonework was found to have completely disintegrated. A gents urinal was situated under the right hand pedestrial archway, in front of which an old character called Billy Turnbull used to shout 'Give us a ha' penny'. (never a penny), which, when it worked, enabled him to buy tobacco at the 'Snuffery' in Tangier Street.

15

15 **Dockside Ephemera, 1888.** This scene will be unfamiliar to anyone less than 88 years old — a view across the docks from Wood Walker's Shipbrokers Offices, upstairs in Tangier Buildings (the old Cocoa Rooms which later became the Co-operative Stores). T.S. Bell's shop was later built on this land. The wall was too prime a site to remain untouched, and John Leathers of Marlborough Street, a long-established Billposter and Bellman (town crier), has seen fit to leave these examples of the Victorian jobbing printer's art for us to savour :—

William Workman of Tangier Street offers Chamber Sets (Jugs and Bowls) for 5/6d and 7/6d. Bowman's tea, at 1/11d per pound is described as the most economical in England! A useful poster for dating purposes tell us that Isle of Man Steamer Packet Company are running special week-end excursions to Ramsay, Isle of Man on Saturday, 30th June, 1888. It seems ironic nowadays, with Concorde and Cumberland Motors, to think that it was quicker to get to the Isle of Man than to Penrith from West Cumberland.

The Broughton Soap Works, Edinburgh, seemed very keen to impress on housewives that their 'Scotsman' Paraffin Laundry Soap at 3d per pound bar was a boon to the housewife, and, we trust, a source of profit for all grocers.

The Whitehaven News were advertising the week's 'scoops', amongst which was "Father Cummins on Orangeism".

The yard seems to have been a boat owners depot with its odd lengths of netting strewn about the roofs.

16 Underneath the lamp post. This is another view from Wood Walker's Offices in 1888, showing the huge coloured theatrical posters for a melodrama playing at the Theatre Royal in Roper Street. The composition of this picture, with its men standing under the gas lamp, the policeman and friend in the middle distance, Captain Mann's house on the right, and the ship's superstructures in the background is remarkably like a theatrical stage set with a painted backdrop.

16

17 Dockside Activity 1900. This is an unusual view of the end of Duke Street and the dockside, taken in 1900. The small building on the right, opposite the baths, advertises Wm. Kennaugh's Chandlers, Sailmakers and Canvas Merchants. The steam crane, No. 3, with its corrugated iron sides, was still operational in the 1940's. The old lamp post, one of many on the dockside, has long since gone, with its familiar lantern top and extending bars, used for supporting the workman's ladder whilst he changed the mantle when it was lit by gas. Though Dick Bewsher tells us that when he was a boy, he always thought they were for swinging on! By the time this photograph was taken, the lamp could well have been electrified, since, by the turn of the century, the public lighting in the town was entirely electric. Whitehaven was a pioneer in public lighting, having had street illumination by oil lamps as far back as January 1781. Gas lighting took over in 1831, and the first electric lights were lit in September 1893.

17

18

18 Coal Horses, 1900. Dockside activity was not just confined to ships and trains. The docks would have been impossible to run without horse power. These heavy horses were used for pulling coal wagons through the coaling station at Queens Dock so that the coal could be dropped through a sluice into ships' holds. The workman is wearing the clothing typical of the time, and best suited to his job, down to the clogs and strings tied round his trousers below the knee.

The sign in the background, (seen better in the two previous photographs) is for the Tedcastle line, which ran steamers to Dublin, Liverpool and Maryport from Whitehaven. Their ships were called *Blackrock, Adela, Eblana, Malay* and *Cumbria*. The S.S. *Cumbria* sailed from Queen's Dock every Wednesday for Dublin, returning via Liverpool every Friday and thence to Whitehaven on Saturday, allowing two days in Dublin and one in Liverpool. The round fare was 20/-.

19   Iron Ore Quay, 1858. This rare photograph shows the original Bulwark — a wooden structure, built before the Queen's Dock, and earlier than the present stone structure of the same name. It was used for loading wagons of iron ore into vessels for shipment to Iron Smelting works in various parts of the country.

19

20   This picture of nautical tranquility was taken about 1890, and shows a local fishing smack, No. WA13, resting up with a smaller boat, 55WA, the *Mayflower*, in the harbour. The port limits were from the river Esk and along the coast to Lowca beck. Fishing boats and their implements are still distinguished by the letters "W.A." In 1905, there were 35 fishing boats registered as belonging to the port, employing 78 men and boys.

20

21   Whitehaven Harbour, 1885.   This is a view of the *Europa*, a fine 3-masted sailing ship. Note the dummy gun ports, made to make a merchant vessel look like a warship from a distance. No Beacon Mills here. The low buildings would be where Kennaugh's sailmakers were established prior to the Beacon Mills being erected. The long, covered, brick-built shed was part of the Whitehaven Junction Railway's buildings. Trains would back up to this shed to facilitate the unloading of luggage straight into the Grand Hotel on the right. The houses on Bransty look clean and new, and, of course, much fewer in number than today.

21

22   Lobster Pots.   This delight-ful composition shows Fisherman McClean on the Old New Quay in the early 1930's, repairing lobster pots before an uninvited audience. Bill Skelly tells us that every time Mr. McClean found a nail on the docks he would pick it up and hammer it into his boat so that it was not wasted. The wooden capstans have all suffered from the effects of weathering and have now gone. During the war, when many a young lad could have shown an interest in the docks, they became a restricted area and were fenced off to keep people out.

22

23   Net Repairs, 1904.   A characteristic, everyday scene on the docks — repairing the net damage from the last trip to ensure a good catch when they next put to sea. The two seamen, one smoking a clay pipe, are seen working by the patent slip, which was situated on the east Strand. It was built by the Earl of Lonsdale in 1870. It admitted four vessels of 150 tons burden, and was so constructed that vessels of any weight could be drawn out of the water and into the shipyard to be repaired.

23

24 Riggers on the *Thirlmere*, 1880. Ropes played a vital role on sailing ships. They were as vital as petrol is to a car if motion was to be achieved. These riggers are doing repairs on the Thirlmere, one of the best known local ships, owned by Fisher and Sproats, a firm who started business in Whitehaven but subsequently moved to Liverpool. Odd lengths of rope can be seen lying around the deck under a vertitable spider's web of rigging. Ropes had always been made at Whitehaven — three manufacturers are listed as being operational in 1847.

24

25

25 On the *Eleanor Dixon*, 1860. This is an early photograph of the Captain and visitors on the ship *Eleanor Dixon*, a frequent visitor to Whitehaven, though not actually built here. Notice the decorated ship's wheel and the wood block grille on which the Captain is standing.

26

26   Lifeboat Men, 1897.   As long as ships have sailed from the town, mariners have tried to make provisions for disasters which can strike boats of all sizes indiscriminately. Whitehaven's lifeboat in the 1890's was the *Elizabeth Leicester*, and this picture shows the Captain with two of the crew members:- Jack and Tom Wignall and Tom Cradduck. Notice their cork life jackets and oiled cloth protective clothing. They are standing in front of the boat, which was mounted on wheels at North Shore for easy launching. A lifeboat was stationed at Whitehaven as early as 1803, long before the founding of the Royal National Lifeboat Institute, and was one of the earliest coastal towns in the country to have its own rescue boat.

27 Inspection Parade. The Whitehaven Volunteer Rocket Launching Brigade, seen here on Inspection Parade on the New Quay in 1889. They paraded before Hugh, Lord Lonsdale, the Yellow Earl. The brigade had attended upwards of 100 wrecks and had saved many lives. The Earl can be seen in front of the Brigade's equipment cart, standing with bowler hat and walking stick. He became the borough's first mayor in 1894. Note the bare footed children to the left and sitting on the wall.

28

28 On Duty. This is a nicely posed shot of one of the Lock Gate Keepers at Queen's Dock Gates. They were operated by inserting poles into the metal capstans, one either side of the gates, and moving the gate with the muscle power of half a dozen men. The gates were widened early in the century to accommodate larger vessels. Note the man's clean clogs and billycock hat.

29

29   The "Hurries".   This lively scene on West Strand shows four coal "hurries" —
metal supported railways over the roadway for speeding the unloading of coal from chaldron wagons into the ships' holds. The building on the left is the Blue Anchor Inn, one of
about 20 public houses which used to line the dock. The Blue Anchor, kept by Kate Ash-
bridge, was situated to the right of Mount Steps. It lost its licence early this century and
became a dwelling house prior to its demolition. It was situated where R. Donnan keeps
his empty fishboxes now.

30

30   When Coal was King, 1904.   This informative postcard, taken from the Old Quay, shows the various levels on which the chaldron wagons travelled to get on to the hurries. A wealth of variety here, dredger, paddle steamer, sailing ship and iron steamer, all here to earn a living from coal by one means or another.

31   Close-up view of a "Hurry", 1910.   This photograph gives us a detailed look at just how the hurry was used and how the coal was directed accurately into the ships' holds. The coal was shipped to the Isle of Man and Ireland, countries which have no coal deposits. The hurries have been down for about 60 years.

31

32

32   Whitehaven Shipyards, 1860.   One of the last wooden vessels to be built at Whitehaven was the *Tennaserim*. It was built in 1860/61, at Brocklebank's Yard and weighed
1,002 tons. It was launched on 10th August, 1861, and had a relatively short career. It
was wrecked in 1865. Twentytwo people can be seen working on the vessel which is
coming along well.

Daniel Brocklebank (1742–1801) was probably the best known local 18th century
ship builder and was the founder of the country's oldest shipping line, the Cunard Line.
He established a yard at Whitehaven in 1782 and built 27 vessels before his death. The
business was carried on by his sons who maintained the yard until 1865. The yard was
closed when the firm decided to go in for iron ships instead of wooden ones which could
not be built locally. 131 vessels were launched from this yard during the last 65 years of
its working existence.

33

33 Across The Harbour, 1880. This pleasant outlook epitomises Whitehaven's principal source of wealth in one photograph — the sea and ships, plus mines and mining. The vessel lying alongside the Old Quay is the *Ulpha*. In the middle distance can be seen a large building from which the local lifeboat was launched, and in the distance is William Pit. On the horizon can just be discerned the old tobacco pipes, or "bacca pipes' as they were colloquially known, where contraband tobacco was burned. Nearby is the old White-haven Infectious Diseases Hospital on Bransty. The vantage point for this picture was Mount Pleasant.

34   Queen's Dock, 1895.   Queen's Dock, named in honour of Queen Victoria, was designed and completed in 1876. This is a view of the S.S. *Sapphire*, an iron, 3-masted steamer of 384 tons built in 1881 by J. Fullerton of Paisley. The ship was owned by Robertson's of Glasgow who had a fleet of ships all named after precious stones, e.g. Pearl and Turquoise. It can be seen here, loading iron ore from specially shaped wagons each with a notch out of the side to help in shovelling the ore down shutes into the hold. The train in the background would shunt the wagons into place for emptying. A large proportion of the locally mined ore was shipped to the various smelting centres in South Wales, Staffordshire and the North East. Note the open wheelhouse on the ship — old sailors must have been a hardy breed!

35   "Come on in! The water isn't cold!"   The docks had more than one use. They made a good place for a refreshing swim on a hot summer day. The corporation baths were only just round the corner in Duke Street. They had only been built 10 years previously when this photograph was taken in 1893. The docks were cheaper and more acceptable if you had no swimming trunks to wear. In summer, swimming exhibitions were held between the piers. This picture is taken at the place known locally as 'the little sands'.

36

36　The road to work.　This is an important and visually very informative picture, taken about 1890, of the road to William Pit. This pit was sunk on the shore below Bransty by Mr. Bateman. Work was begun in 1804 and completed in 1812. The first coal was shipped from it in 1806. The miners, seen here on their way to work, have their back-bottles slung over their shoulders. These soldered tin bottles were made by John Lowther and sold by Herdman's in the Market Place. They cost about 1/6d and were for carrying drinks to the coal face in the pre-vacuum flask era. This road, for many families, is a road of anguish and sorrow, for mine disasters were not uncommon, and many men and boys walked to work along this road only to be carried back. William Pit's worst moment was in 1947 when 117 men were killed. The mine ceased production in 1955 and the site was later levelled.

　　The gas company's works, seen on the left of the picture, were built on the site of old shipyards. They sold gas coke which was cheaper than elsewhere and you could go and buy it from them by the pramload. The gasworks came down several years ago. Nothing seen in this picture, other than the roadway, survives.

37

37   A break for tea. This is a view of the Screen Lasses in the grub house at William Pit in 1910. Mary Jane McCourt is 3rd from the left, and 'Aunt' Jane Law is seated on the right wearing her bonnet. Their work was hard and dirty, picking metal and pieces of stone out of the coal as it passed them on a conveyor belt. They worked in a draughty metal-roofed shed. The noise was loud and continuous and many ladies learnt to lip read in order to be able to understand one another whilst they worked. They did not wear gloves, but occasionally wore mits in winter. Daughter followed mother into the job. Many left to have families and returned when the children were old enough to be left. This job only ceased locally in February 1970. When the work ended at Haig Pit the longest serving ladies were :– Miss Mary Jane McNulty with 32 years unbroken service, Mrs. M. J. Taggerty with 31 years in two spells and Mrs. B. Oldfield with 23 years service.

38

38 Ancient 'corves' at William Pit, 1875. About 1675, corves were introduced into West Cumbrian mines for the conveyance of coal from the workings to the surface. The first recorded mention of them was in the pay sheets of Green Bank Colliery in that year. The corf was a circular basket made of hazel rods, provided with an iron bow for attachment to the hook at the end of the winding rope. The first corves carried 2½cwt. each, but the size of the corf increased as larger pits were sunk and when the horse gins were replaced by steam winding engines. They were discontinued in the Newcastle area as early as 1834, but continued to be used locally at William Pit until 1875, when they were superceded by steel tubs. Before being discontinued, the corves were carrying loads of up to 12cwt. each. At the surface, the baskets were lowered onto small, wheeled bogies for transport to the screens for sorting.

39

39　Free Coal!　Mary Ellen Spence lived in old Peter Street, and can be seen here in 1920 in front of William Pit with the results of her coal picking labours gathered on the beach. It was hard work and the bags were very heavy, especially when you had no transport other than your own back. Note the way the bag is balanced on the small of the back with a rope to steady it. The square pit chimney was the subject of a petition to save it in 1970, but the Coal Board said it was unsafe and demolished it.

40 The price of coal. This is a picture of 14 of the many brave and selfless men who volunteered to go down Wellington Pit after the gas explosion and subsequent fires which caused the greatest single loss of life that the town has ever suffered when 136 men and boys were killed on 11th May, 1910.

These men, with 'Mecco' breathing apparatus, went down the mine on recovery work at great personal risk to bring out the casualties. The tall man, 3rd from the right on the back row, was Tommy Quayle, delegate at William Pit.

40

41 This is another photograph showing the breathing apparatus in situ before the men went down the shaft. Note the size of the wooden chaldron wagons, the term "chaldron" being used to denote 36 bushels.

41

42

42   Road repairs, 1910.   This is a grand sight — a machine with a heart! This photograph shows road repairs about 1910 in George Street at the corner of Scotch Street. The driver of the open topped steamroller was old Tom Bell, and the chap with the rake was 'La'll Newcastle Tommy' Pye. The road roller was probably an Aveling and Porter machine made at Rochester. This type of machine was first introduced in 1878. It had driving wheels of 7ft. in diameter and 16" wide on the face, constructed of a specially strong section of tee iron. The machine's boiler worked at a pressure of 150lbs. per square inch. The working parts of the engine were neatly boxed in and the fly wheel was of the solid disc pattern so as not to frighten horses. The steamroller was in existence up to a few years ago, when Hanratty demolished it in the Corporation Yard on instructions from Borough Engineer, Arthur Wilson.

43

43   Running repairs.   This rare photograph shows the Lady Margaret, one of a quartet of very well known char-a-bancs owned by T. Meageen's Whitehaven Motor Transport Ltd. Mr. Meageen was the pioneer of Motor transport in West Cumberland and he left a thriving legacy called Cumberland Motor Services when he died in 1941. The 'charas' were all 1920 model new 40 h.p. torpedo-de-luxe bodies, luxuriously upholstered with roll seats and full curved spring backs. The other three were named Lady Betty, Lady Mary and Lady Grace. The tyres were solid and the canvas top was folded back in warm weather. The firm ran a 'Lady Betty Holiday Savings Club', in which one could save up for day tours to Lakeland, or 8-day tours of Scotland. The buses ran daily throughout the locality, and were eventually shipped to Douglas, Isle of Man, where they were used on the promenade.

44 Water Cart, 1895. The road surface in the town at the turn of the century was a McAdamed one, which was quite adequate for the volume of traffic. In summer the corporation water cart would go through the streets spraying water, to keep down the dust — usually followed by a flock of giggling children running in and out of the water spray. This view of the Castle with its high walls is obviously taken in summer. The trees are rich in foliage, and the lady is using her umbrella as a parasol to ward off the strong rays of the sun. Behind the lady can be seen the doorway to the gatekeeper's lodge. The chimneys on the Castle have since been removed because they let in water. The house now looks much more like a traditional 'castle' without them.

45   The New Houses, 1927.   These 'New' Houses looked down onto Preston Street. They were built in 1788 by a former Lord Lonsdale for the use of his men and labourers. The rent-free terraced houses were built on the side of a hill and formed three rows or streets. The roofs were level with the roadway of the upper terraces so that children could run along the roofs, peer down the skylights or drop things down the chimneys. The top row was built full against the hillside. No sewers, drains or running water taps were built in originally. Over 500 houses had been planned, but only 260 were actually built. The middle row, seen here, was the longest, with 111 houses and 9 ashpits — a primitive form of sewage disposal arrangement. "There was not a single privy for the whole property" notes the 1849 Health Report. Many people died of typhus fever, small-pox and tuberculosis as a result of living in these houses which were constantly damp. The rows were sewered with yellow pottery sewer pipes in the 1860's and the outside closets can be seen in the picture. The building on the near right, the only one still standing though partly filled in, was a kind of dispensary/ambulance station. Its Gothic shaped windows and castellated top are more reminiscent of a monastery — not surprising when there was no new style of architecture for this type of building and the only examples to date were run by religious orders. The large building on the left horizon was Ben Fidler's Corn Merchants and the building behind is Christ Church. The former has been demolished and the church's future is now uncertain. The cobbled roadway is still discernable under the overgrown foliage. These houses were pulled down in 1939, though some of the lower ones remained until a later date. The occupants were rehoused 'en masse' at Greenbank in houses with modern amenities but costing rather more than the 10d per fortnight which is what these old houses cost to rent.

46 Mount Steps and Magarry's Houses on West Strand, 70 years ago. One cannot imagine that building land was so scarce in early Victorian times that developments such as this had to take place. It looks just like an illustration from Doré's views of Dickensian London. The steps originally ran up both sides, but were cobbled over when they fell into disrepair. There are 18 people in this picture, which is only a small fraction of the actual inhabitants, being only the mothers and small children, the rest of the families being out at school or work. The houses were demolished many years ago and the occupants rehoused. The steps were re-modelled about 7 years ago, leaving the lower storeys of the house walls still standing with bricked-up doors and windows. The remnants of the iron window bars of the first house on the right can still be seen. The building on the left, the Central Electric Lighting Station still stands. There was something grimly facetious about the name Mount Pleasant when one had to get to it past scenes such as this.

46

47 "Seldom Seen" (but often mentioned). This old house near Coalgrove Bank Farm, seen here in 1905, was situated in a little valley to the left and below the level of the road to St. Bees. The road's boundary wall can be seen in the background. The opening at the bottom of the picture is where the beck came out of a pipe. A bearmouth entrance to a coalmine was accessible through a passageway covered by an iron grille which is just visible as a black mark on the house wall by the little boy's shoulder, one of the group seated on the right. The house was last lived in by a family called Mossop and was pulled down about 40 years ago.

47

48

49

48 & 49 Old Pals, 1888. The history behind this photograph is rather interesting. A photographer saw these two characters, Duck Foot Charlie Smith and Geordie Mitchell, shaking hands on the dock following their conversion by the Salvation Army (alas, only for a brief period), and, grasping the opportunity of taking an inconventional picture, invited them into his studio.

Charlie Smith (L) lived in West Strand. He joined the navy and served for a considerable period before he had the misfortune to lose his left foot. This proved a great handicap to him but he managed to eke out a precarious living by 'hobbling' (no pun intended). Hobblers assisted vessels coming into port by carrying ropes run out from the ship to the quay. They also used to help in furling the sails, though being lame, Charlie was unable to go aloft. Charlie died about 1910. Hobbling, a coveted job on the dock is still carried on today by Benny Quayle.

Geordie Mitchell, also a native of West Strand, had no fixed abode for many years. He joined the army but found discipline irksome and was dismissed whilst serving in India. After discharge, he returned to the town, and managed to find the odd day's work now and again loading and unloading steamers etc. at the Sugar Tongue. He often appeared in court for sleeping rough, as can be seen in the lower picture on the opposite page, taken in the Green Market. He lived to the age of 80 in spite of it all.

50 Matthew Piper, Philanthropist. This portrait is of a man, well known by reputation in Whitehaven, who died before the invention of photography. He was a quaker who died in 1820 aged 91, leaving various legacies which have helped many families in the town for over 150 years. His best known charity was to leave £50, being the interest on £1,000 to provide the poor with nourishing soup in the winter months. The Soup Kitchen was situated originally in Queen Street, but has been operated from 1, Mill Street since 1867. In its heyday, it provided up to 100 gallons of soup twice weekly — Wednesday and Saturday. It now provides soup and bread for 50 people, which is all delivered. The committee is composed of the wives of professional businessmen in the town. The original fund was not sufficient to keep pace with 20th century inflation and has been generously supplemented from other sources.

Mr. Piper also founded a Marine School in High Street, in 1817 "for the education of sixty poor boys resident in the town of Whitehaven or the neighbourhood in reading, writing, arithmetic, guageing, navigating and book keeping". The school was endowed with £2,000 and opened in 1822. Before being admitted, the boys had to be able to read the New Testament, and none were allowed to remain for more than five years. The education was designed to instruct boys for positions of mates and mariners of vessels, though ironically, they were not under any obligation to go to sea. School facilities improved in the area and the Old Marine School was sold, and in 1908 the money was used to purchase the site of the Old Grammar School, now Richmond School, a building whose own future has been uncertain.

51   Aviation Pioneer.   This is a rare snap taken when Colonel Cody landed at Whitehaven on 31st July, 1911, whilst participating in the Daily Mail Curcuit of Britain, £10,000 Air Race. He was forced to make an emergency landing because of very strong head winds during his flight from Carlisle to Manchester en route for the finish at Brooklands. He tried to land his biplane *The Flying Cathedral* on the site of the Roman Fort at Moresby but found it impossible and moved on to Aikbank where he found a suitable field at Hunting How

Farm and landed there at 5.30 a.m. The biplane was roped off by the police and hundreds of people turned up to see it, many of them sneaking out of work to do so. Colonel Cody dined at Moresby Hall whilst waiting for his mechanics to arrive by road from Windermere. After being repaired, the plane left and flew on to Manchester, Worcester, Bristol and Weston Super Mare. The race lasted from 22nd July to 1st August and out of a field of 22, he came in 4th, only a day behind the 3rd place pilot. His was the only biplane to complete the course.

52   Barney the Goose was Whitehaven's best loved character and probably one of the best selling post card subjects. There are at least 4 views of this bird whose fame rested on its amazing ability to drink beer from a glass. Its owner, seen in the middle resting his leg on a timber beam was Billy Bell. The man with the walrus moustache was 'Old Morris'.

This picture was taken in 1904. The goose lived to be 16 years of age and was killed by a dog. Poems were written lamenting his death. People left money at Miss Hartley's Coffee House in Duke Street to provide the goose with its daily buns and cakes, since the goose called there every day.

52

53

53 Sonny Blaney the 'Sawdust King', seen here in 1930, on his cart with his well known white horse called 'Lie-a-bed'. Sonny lived with his wife Kate and family in Queen Street, and for a living he sold bags of sawdust which he acquired from the timber yard and the pit top. It was used on butchers shop floors and in public houses. He had bad eyesight and people often played pranks with his transport. 'Spike' McLaughlin tells us that when Sonny was in Dalzell's butchers delivering one day, someone moved the position of his cart in the street, exchanging it for Dalzell's own cart which also had a white horse. It was only when he started delivering further up the Market that he realized he had a cart-load of meat. On other occasions the wags would unhitch his horse and turn it round in the shafts with its tail facing forwards and Lie-a-bed licking the driver's face. A man fortunate enough to own a horse and cart was always in work because he could hire himself out for all kinds of light carting and removal jobs.

54   This gentleman is Stephen McAleavy, known locally as 'Leatherlugs'. He was a local character who wandered around the district, with his bag over his shoulder, selling 'reddening' and 'sill', preparations for decorating the front doorsteps of houses. A spotless threshold was every housewife's aim because it reflected the state of the house inside. He constantly muttered expletives about the iron ore miners of Cleator Moor and the state of finances in Whitehaven shops. Children used to taunt him and he had a wild temper when roused. Parents used him as a verbal deterrent to misbehaving children by exclaiming 'If you don't behave, I'll let Leatherlugs get you!'.

54

55   On the ball.   This is an appropriate picture to include in this age of Women's Lib. The Whitehaven Ladies' Amateur Football Team are seen here in 1917. They played for charity on Saturday afternoons at the Cricket Ground and were very good players. They even beat Dick Kerr's Ladies from Preston — a team considered to be the finest in the country.

55

56 Roan's, 14/15 Roper Street, 1900. John Roan was the largest leather goods manufacturer in the county. He made Harness, Saddles, Machine Belting, Travelling Bags, Trunks, Portmanteaux and Hat Cases. Mr. Roan is standing, hand on hip in the shop doorway with 13 members of his staff. The business had been originally Brownrigg Taylor's Drysalters, and Mr. Roan took over the premises in the 1890's. There is an air of activity about the place, which one would expect when one equates saddles and harnesses for the horsedrawn age as being the equivalent of producing tyres for cars to-day. The decoration on the walls gives the place a continental look. The firm also had branches at Workington and Cockermouth. Burnyeats took over in the 1920's and in 1974 vacated the property to move into Peter Leech's Grocery establishment on Lowther Street to make way for site redevelopment.

56

58 Smiling service. This is a sight to gladden the heart of any old grocer and, indeed, anyone who prefers personal service rather than self selection. Walter Willson's Cash Grocers at No. 71 Market Place. This scene, taken about 1905, shows the manager, Mr. Law, standing in the doorway with his staff. The white overalls were very practical, especially when one considers that everything was sold loose and had to be cut and weighed out e.g. butter on special offer at 1/- per lb., middle bacon at 4d per lb., ham at 6d per lb. Quaker Oats were 3½d and 5½d a packet. The faceted lamp over the door, a common practise over Victorian shops, illuminates the word 'TEA', which was a real stand-by in those days, as a meal of tea, bread and marg was quite common, and the kettle was usually boiling on the hob, ready for unexpected visitors. The shop eventually moved round onto the frontage formerly occupied by the Cocoa Rooms and Billy Wilson, the butcher moved into the shop which faced the Market Hall. The butcher's shop is now at Cleator Moor and Walter Willson's considerably extended the shop inside about 7 years ago.

57   Local Pottery, 1900.   This is a rare view of workers at Patman's Earthenware Pottery at the top of Coach Road. Its principal manufacture was heavy domestic brownware pottery decorated with cream lines — bread crocks, salt pots, baking dishes etc. The clay was dug out of the hillside at Monkwray and transported by cart to Meadow View, where it was dropped through a hole in the wall, into the pottery yard. The cart was driven by Jack 'Docky' Nicholson in the early part of the century. Mr. Patman died in 1910, but the business continued until 1915 under the direction of Mr. Patman's foreman, William Thornber.

59   Wilson and Kitchin were very well known in the area for their many and diverse manufactures. They were wholesale and retail chemists, druggists and drysalters at No. 27 King Street. This view, taken about 1905, shows the very large windows with their glass carboys filled with coloured water, the pharmacists symbol. The firm had stores in various parts of the town. They sold paint, and manufactured whiting, cement, chemical manure, bath bricks etc. One of their warehouses, the oil and paint store, was the old Guinea Warehouse, situated opposite the Market Place end of Irish Street. It was an ancient warehouse built in the early 1700's, its name being taken from the time when Whitehaven was doing trade with the Guinea Coast. It was gutted by fire in September 1928. Among the many things they manufactured was 'Wilkin's Tic Mixture'. The shop in King Street is now the site of Woodhouse's Furnishers.

60

60   Early Motoring. This building will be well known to most people – T.S. Bell's Electrical Shop in Tangier Street. The property, built at an angle from the rest of the buildings in the street, was built at the turn of the century by H.S. Jacques and was a garage in the early days of motoring. Compare the site above with what it looked like in 1888 on page 14. A smart new shop with well filled windows, informative writing on the wall, together with an example of the cars they repaired. The business altered its emphasis to electrical work when it passed over to T.S. Bell, their electrician, on the death of Mr. Jacques.

61 & 62   The Flour Mills.   These two pictures depict what must have been Whitehaven's largest brick built building — John Pattinson's Beacon Mills, seen under construction in 1907, and later in 1909 when it had been completed. John Pattinson originally
had two water mills at Penrith. The business moved to Whitehaven in 1885 to the Barrack
Mills in Catherine Street. It ran its own ships and became a limited company in 1906. The
Beacon Mills were built on the old Shipyard site by A. & T. Anderson, local builders. It
was taken over by Quaker Oats Ltd. in 1949 and was sold and demolished in 1975. It
would have made a good office block for someone — a large building, with good parking
facilities and a particularly pleasant outlook. Ironic that a building which looked as
though it would last a 1,000 years had a life span shorter than the average human.

63 Market Place under water, 1906. Flooding in the Market Place was, and still is, due to a combination of things — high tides, lots of rain making the Pow Beck full, and a westerly equinoxial wind pushing the sea into shore. Old people tell us that floods happened several times a year, and that rowing a boat up to the Y.M.C.A. in Irish Street was not unheard of. The shops in the picture are sandbagged even today when high tides are expected.

63

64 The biggest bonfire in England — 1911. It was a national habit at the turn of the century to build bonfires to celebrate Royal occasions. Whitehaven entered into the spirit of things with relish and produced this monster for the coronation of George V. It was 130 feet 6 inches high, 150 feet in circumference, octagonal in shape and had a circumference of 20 feet at the top. For a height of 80 feet it was built solid of pit props and sleepers, and the upper portion of lighter material :— several tiers of tar barrels, brushwood and shavings. An air shaft 7 feet square ran up the middle with a ladder from top to bottom. It was surmounted by a 28 foot pine tree, and the whole structure was steadied by guyropes. The material it contained weighed 600 tons and were soaked by 2000 gallons of petrol. It was built with materials supplied by Whitehaven Colliery Co. and Lord Lonsdale at Low Road, behind the Laundry. The bonfire was lit by Alderman Deas at 10pm on June 22nd 1911. It was claimed to be the largest in England, a claim that remained unchallenged though 1564 others were built. If one counts the tree in the height, its nearest rival, built at Farringdon near Exeter was 60 feet shorter. In 1902, Whitehaven had built another record breaker for Edward VII's Coronation 120 feet 4 inches high at Arrowthwaite; the main difference in height being the tree on top. It is interesting to note that the tradition of bonfires is to be revived for the Queen's Silver Jubilee in 1977 — will Whitehaven excel itself again?

64

65 The Tannery Fire, 23rd March, 1908. This is a view of firemen damping down at Wm. Walker's Tannery. The works were situated in High Street and Scotch Street. The noticeable feature was a wooden sided footbridge over the street joining the premises on either side. We take candid action photography for granted today, but this view of men at work is very uncommon and a tribute to Mr. Bellman's skill as a photographer. The corporation fire brigade was situated in Scotch Street and the Captain was J. W. White, who had a complement of 2 officers and 17 men. In 1864, the fire brigade was composed of the whole of the police force, rather than specific firemen, which would explain why the old fire station was sited next door to the police station.

66 Basket House, 1968. Situated at Prospect, this was originally a place where baskets were made in Whitehaven for the pits. It was the subject of a demolition order in 1969, and the former town Librarian, Mr. Hay, tried to prevent its demolition. A petition was signed by 446 people but without success. It was lived in latterly by three generations of the Telford family and was a small grocery shop until it was demolished.

67

67   The Grand Hotel Fire.   The largest and most imposing building in the centre of the town, known as the Grand, was an hotel, situated immediately in front of the railway station at Bransty. It was a large building erected in 1846/47 by the Earl of Lonsdale, at immense expense, to Italianate designs by Mr. Barnes of London, and built by Hugh Todhunter of Whitehaven. It was originally called the Lonsdale Hotel and covered an area of 6,000 square feet — 100 feet in length and 60 feet wide. It had eighty rooms including a spacious ballroom, large public coffee room of more than 1,200 square feet etc. There was a footbridge from the station to the hotel by which luggage could be speedily removed for travellers alighting from trains. The hotel suffered in the depression, being such a big building to keep running. The building had been palatial in its heyday, but, built as it was, in the pre-electric age and when plumbing was a luxury, there were no provisions for modern amenities. Jugs of hot water had to be brought round in the morning for washing and shaving etc. It caught fire on 21st January, 1940, and this is the only photograph taken whilst it was burning. A Miss Taylor died in the blaze. The photograph was taken from Bransty Hill.

68   This is a picture of the Grand Hotel being demolished on 29th March, 1941. The columned portico with the ladder in front, was the Main Entrance to the building. Horse drawn coaches would come round the corner from the left and turn in a wide circle to drop passengers at the door.

69   This picture, taken a fortnight later on 12th April, 1941, shows the progress made by the demolishers. The stone finialled building on the left was the Cuckoo Bar. The structure remained at this level for several years until it was acquired by Cumberland Motors for garaging 'buses. The lower portion of the walls can still be seen by the observant pedestrian, even in 1976.

68

69

51

70

70   The Town Hall, October, 1939. War against Germany was declared on Sunday, 3rd September, 1939, by Neville Chamberlain. It was a time of extreme uncertainty and everyone thought the country would be bombed. This picture, taken three weeks later, shows the precautions taken by the Council to protect the Town Hall by covering all the entrances with sandbags. Notice the railings which gave the building a greater sense of proportion.

71   A Royal Visitor.   Prince George, the Duke of Kent, visited the town on 3rd July, 1941. He went through the town to a reception at the Town Hall, accompanied by the Mayor, Alderman J.B. Smith. Here the Duke can be seen wearing the uniform of a Group Commander of the Royal Air Force outside the Town Hall. He talked to widows and mothers who had been bereaved in a recent explosion at William Pit, in which 12 men lost their lives. He also inspected a parade of A.R.P. girls. The Prince died in an aeroplane crash before the war ended.

71

72

72　After the final curtain.　　This is one of a couple of rare photographs taken inside
the old Theatre Royal in Roper Street about 20 years ago, before the building was demolished. The theatre had been operative on the site since 1769. In 1847, one observer stated,
'The taste for dramatic literature has been for some time on the decline in this town,
owing perhaps in some measure, to the rare appearance of any theatrical luminary, and
the present lack of talent introduced'.

　　The original interior was modelled on a theatre built at Bath, another fine Georgian
town. Whitehaven's theatrical history really started in Howgill Street at the Assembly
Rooms, opened in 1736 by John Hayton, who subsequently built an annexe which was
used for theatrical performances. The earliest surviving playbill dates from 14th January,
1756, a comedy entitled *The Suspicious Husband*. In 1767, Watson's Assembly Rooms
opened in Albion Street as a theatre but did not survive long after the Theatre Royal
opened.

73

73   The Theatre Royal suffered latterly along with many other theatres with the coming of moving pictures and cinemas. For a time, short films were shown in between variety acts in an attempt to retain their popularity, but it was not a success. The best remembered manager of later years was Stanley Rogers who made many improvements to the property and who was responsible for bringing repertory, musical play, thrillers, variety shows and opera to the town. The building was closed in 1930 because it did not conform to the statutory regulations with regard to exits and the licence was not renewed. The building was auctioned in Manchester at the Midland Hotel, when it was withdrawn after only one bid of £1,300. Seven years later it was acquired by the Whitehaven News and used as a store prior to its demolition. The site was redeveloped as a printing works which is now empty since the paper has been acquired by the Cumberland News Group and printing operations moved to Lillyhall and Carlisle.

74   Meadow View, 1965.   This is the entrance and frontage of the Whitehaven Union Workhouse, built on St. Bees Road in 1854/55 at a cost of £8,000, to accommodate 424 persons. It was built as a refuge for the old, impoverished and destitute in the days before Social Security Benefits. In 1905, an Infirmary wing was added with beds for 75 inmates. The building was T-shaped with a tower at the crux, just visible behind the central chimneys. It was renamed Meadow View House between the wars to get away from its workhouse stigma, and was used as a long-stay geriatric hospital in the years prior to its closure. In the early 1960's, subsidence due to mine workings caused the building to become unsafe, and it was vacated and sold to the Corporation for demolition and proposed redevelopment which never took place. It covered an area of 3 acres and there were 4 acres of gardens.

74

75

75   The Old Citadel.   This building in Catherine Street, formerly the Wesleyan Association Chapel, was built in the reign of William IV in 1836 at a cost of £1,700. It could accommodate 600 persons and a Sunday School was situated behind it. It was taken over by the Salvation Army as a Citadel early this century after spells in James Street and Duke Street and was used continuously by them until 1970/71 when it was demolished. A new purpose built citadel was erected on the site, which opened in October 1971.

76

76 'If only we had a penny'.   This beautiful example of a Georgian shop window,
with its curved front and delicate window tracery was situated in George Street. The shop
facade seen here just before the war, was only demolished about 7 years ago. It was used
as a little general grocer's shop selling everything from paraffin to sweets, and was one of
only 4 remaining Georgian shop windows in the town. Shops dating from this period were
almost always dwelling houses with shop fronts inserted into them. A building built as a
shop was a great rarity. One has only to look at shop premises in Lowther Street to see
that most of the upper storeys were originally domestic premises.

77 Cleator Moor Railway Station, 1905. A typical Victorian railway station, built in 1857 by Dickenson and Sons of Egremont, it was situated adjacent to the main Whitehaven — Cleator Moor road. The Whitehaven, Cleator and Egremont Railway suffered financially when the Cleator and Workington Junction Railway was opened. In the 20th century, too, the railway's business also suffered with the advent of a regular bus service. The station was demolished about 7 years ago and the lines taken up. A new housing development is nearing completion on the site.

78 The Iron Works at Cleator Moor, 1910. There have been Iron Works in the area since the early 1700's. The original works were situated on the site of the old Linen Thread Mills at Cleator. The furnaces in the picture were built by the Whitehaven Iron and Steel Co. and were first erected in 1841. In 1883 they had 5 furnaces, turning out about 1,000 tons a week. Two events which gave great impetus to the iron industry were the invention of the Bessemer Process in 1856 and the construction of the Whitehaven, Cleator and Egremont Railway about 1857. Prior to the opening of this railway the ore had to be carted to Whitehaven and packed in depots to await shipment. But even this was a great advance upon the days when the metal was carried from the mine to the sea on the backs of ponies and over rough unmade tracks. The Iron Works were taken down earlier this century and the levelled area became an industrial factory site.

78

79   Leconfield Street, 1904. This row of neat sandstone cottages is known locally as 'Cogglety'. The horse drawn Co-operative cart can be seen going past Hutchinson's Cycle Works situated opposite St. John's Church. The building was erected in 1857 as a School by the Haematite Iron Company of Cleator Moor, under the headship of John Rooke, an artist who lived at Keekle Grove. The school came to an end in 1886. It had two storeys, the upper one being reached by an

outside staircase. Notice the original bell tower. Jacob Hutchinson's Motor and Bicycle Depot ceased business in 1915 and the building was turned into 3 dwelling houses. The baby seated on the steps of the lower end house is Mrs. Mary Rooney, who has lived in the house since she was born, and who kindly lent us this photograph.

80   Post Haste! This splendid picture shows Charlie Hutchinson of the Bicycle and Motor Depot, driver of the Royal Mail Van, in 1905. This must have been one of the first Mail Vans — the Edward VII monogram can clearly be seen painted on the side. Notice the solid tyres, chain drive and starting handle fixed on the side rather than the front of the vehicle. The driving apparel was obviously designed to combat the elements, since the open cab would not afford much protection.

81 Montreal Schools, 1906 The school was erected by John Stirling, Esq., J.P. in 1865, and enlarged in 1875. The impressive building had a fine tower 98 feet high containing a clock and bell. The school held 810 children and employed a staff of 26 teachers. Just after the war, in 1946, cracks started to appear in the walls of the school which consequently had to close down. The damage was caused by subsidence at Crowgarth Mine which also affected the houses in Montreal Street. The cracks in the walls of the terraced houses grew so wide that you could dip your bread into your next door neighbour's gravy! The mine workings were so close to the surface that miners could hear horses and carts overhead in High Street. There was no worry about the time whilst underground, since the school clock could clearly be heard chiming. The cracks in the walls became worse through shotfiring and eventually both the street and this magnificent school had to be demolished as they were sinking into the ground. This view was taken before the Employment Exchange was built on a site where these children are sitting.

82 William McLean, hairdresser, tobacconist and authorised emigration agent, 1 Jacktrees Road, and 50 High Street, about 1900. This large building at the corner of Cleator Moor Square was a familiar sight with its highly decorated walls — a fine example of local signwriting. Many locals booked their passage to America or South Africa from here when the bottom dropped out of the Iron Ore industry. Unemployment and its resultant hardship rose dramatically and forced many men to look for mining work in other parts of the world.

82

83 In 1921, a severe fire gutted the building on the corner of Jacktrees Road — McLean's tobacconists, McCartney's Butchers, Slater's Milliners and Grayson's Chemists shop. The buildings on the right became unsafe and were demolished. Rushton's drapers who occupied premises round the corner on High Street, also owned the Grayson property and by mutual arrangement, McClean's was transferred to this site at No. 4 Jacktrees Road, where it is still in business today.

84

84 Cleator Moor Square, 1905. There are very few towns in the county which can boast such a spacious and well laid out square. In this picture we can see the Cocoa Rooms at 10, High Street, owned by Whitehaven Cocoa and Coffee House Co. Ltd., of Tangier Street. The little shops beyond, now a Chinese Cafe, were H. Simpson's Hairdressers at No. 11 and Thos. Scott's Fishmongers at 12, High Street. The Stirling Monument has since been moved to a site between the Library and Office Buildings. Thomas Fowles, Clothier and Draper, 48, High Street is now part of the Co-operative Society buildings.

85

85 Hoarding on Jacktrees Road. After the Jacktrees Road fire, the property was boarded up and became a hoarding for Mr. McLean's emigration and travel posters. The posters for Cunard and White Star Lines, both, incidentally, Cumbrian firms, advertise 3rd Class Cabin returns to Canada and U.S.A. from £35. The cigarette machine blocking the doorway to Emily Slater's old millinery shop dispensed cigarettes at 6d for ten and 1/- for twenty. Surprisingly, the authors have recently seen an identical machine, still operating, in Main Street, Wigton.

86 Heathcotes Foundry, Birks Road, about 1900. Heathcote's were principally engaged in engineering, boilermaking and brassfounding. Their works, sited by the railway lines in Birks Road were much involved with the local mining industry at Cleator Moor. They repaired locomotives and wagons, sold and hired boring machinery, had a 12 inch locomotive for hire and were agents for Muxlow and Knott's Jumper Steel! The entire staff, seen here with their founder, Mr. Heathcote, bearded and standing on the left of the middle row. The firm was taken over by Rylan Engineering of Heysham in 1974 and its rather uncertain future now seems assured. The original building was formerly an old barn.

86

87 The Church of Our Lady of the Sacred Heart, Cleator, 1869. This rare photograph shows the laying of the foundation stone on 3rd October, 1869. All morning it had poured with rain, but fortunately it stopped before the ceremony at 2 p.m. One shilling was charged for admission within the walls, which were several feet high when the foundation stone was laid by Bishop James Chadwick of Hexham and Newcastle. It was opened on 23rd June, 1872. The beautiful Gothic building was designed by E. Welby Pugin, the celebrated Victorian architect. It seated 1,000 people and cost £6,000 to build. This was the second Catholic church to be built at Cleator. The first St. Mary's was built in 1853 by Father Holden, for the English Benedictines on half an acre called Priest Croft purchased from Mr. Jenkinson of Todholes. This building later became a school, but it is now closed.

88

88   Ennerdale Road Mission, 1908.   This postcard photograph was meant to show off the Ennerdale Road Mission Church at Wath Brow. The building, which seats 300 was built of local stone in 1881 and is served by St. John's Church. It is superbly sited at the T-junction, and has been painted by many artists including L. S. Lowry. It is ironic that the picture looks rather more like an advertisement for a brewery since there are two draymen in the picture delivering beer barrels to the Rising Sun and the Greyhound Inns.

89   Main Street Cleator, about 1905.   This scene has altered very little over the years. The costume — long skirts, white aprons, flat caps and clogs may have gone, but the strongly built sandstone terraces, still stand. The buildings reflect the close knit nature and community identity of the people. After all, this is not Cleator Moor, but Cleator, a settlement quite separate, and with much older roots.

89